Yasser ARAFAT

Whitefish Bay Public Library

D A T E   D U E

FL-28-2

Biography

Yasser ARAFAT

George Headlam

Lerner Publications Company
Minneapolis

This book is available in two editions:
Library binding by Lerner Publications Company,
    a division of Lerner Publishing Group
Soft cover by First Avenue Editions,
    an imprint of Lerner Publishing Group
241 First Avenue North
Minneapolis, MN 55401 U.S.A.

Website address: www.lernerbooks.com

Library of Congress Cataloging-in-Publication Data

Headlam, George.
    Yasser Arafat / by George Headlam.
        p.   cm. — (A&E biography)
    Includes bibliographical references and index.
    ISBN: 0–8225–5004–0 (lib. bdg. : alk. paper)
    ISBN: 0–8225–9902–3 (pbk. : alk. paper)
    1. Arafat, Yasser, 1929—Juvenile literature. 2. Palestinian National
Authority—Biography—Juvenile literature. 3. Munaòzòzamat
al-Taòhràir al-Filasòtàinàiyah—Presidents—Biography—Juvenile
literature. I. Title. II. Biography (Lerner Publications Company)
DS126.6.A67 H43 2004
956.95'3044'092—dc092   2002013957

Manufactured in the United States of America
1 2 3 4 5 6 – JR – 09 08 07 06 05 04

CONTENTS

Yasser Arafat, trapped in his Ramallah headquarters by the Israeli army, March 29, 2002. With electricity cut off, he used candlelight to handle paperwork.

Chapter **ONE**

THE FATHER OF PALESTINE

IT WAS MARCH 2002. THE LOCATION WAS Ramallah in the West Bank, a piece of Middle Eastern land west of the Jordan River and the Dead Sea. The West Bank is hotly disputed. It has been fought over and claimed by many different countries and peoples of different religions, including Jews, Christians, and Muslims, for thousands of years. It has been part of Jewish kingdoms, the Roman Empire, the Islamic Ottoman Empire, and a British mandate. In the 2000s, the Israeli government claims rights over most of it. Since 1994 parts of the West Bank have been governed by the Palestinian Authority, the official government of the Palestinian people.

For two months, tanks and armored cars surrounded

a compound in Ramallah—the headquarters of one man. His name is Yasser Arafat. As the leader of the Palestinians, Arafat is a hero to many of his people. As an accused terrorist, he is wanted by Israel's government.

Israeli troops surrounded Arafat's compound that March. Arafat could not safely leave the compound. If he left on foot, he might be shot. If he left by car, his vehicle motorcade might be fired upon. He could not leave by air, because his three helicopters had been destroyed the previous December. The Israeli government said that it would offer Arafat a safe passage out of his headquarters—but only if he left the country altogether. Arafat did not accept the offer.

The Israeli authorities tried another tactic: they tried to make life very uncomfortable for the inhabitants of the compound. They temporarily cut off the electricity and water. They would not allow food supplies to be brought in. They cut the land phone lines. Without electricity, it was impossible to charge up cell phones, so it was no longer possible to communicate with the outside world.

By the end of the month, Israel was exerting more pressure. Troops took over most of the compound. Arafat was holed up in an office on the second floor with two aides. Two tanks were stationed at the bottom of the stairs. Arafat responded to Israeli prime minister Ariel Sharon's offer of permanent exile by saying that he would rather die than leave the West Bank.

An Israeli tank shell explodes inside Arafat's Ramallah headquarters on March 29, 2002, in an unsuccessful attempt to force Arafat out.

Yasser Arafat is someone who is used to getting out of very difficult situations. Over the past four decades, he has survived several assassination attempts. This time, too, he was sure that sooner or later he would find a way out. One more month passed, until the U.S. government persuaded the Israeli government to end the blockade.

A LIFE OF CONFLICT

Yasser Arafat has lived all his life fighting. He has fought in wars. Many people call him a terrorist fighter. To others, he has been a fighter for a cause. Yasser Arafat's cause is to create an independent state for the world's five million Palestinian people. They live in parts of the West Bank and Gaza over which the

After Arafat's release from the blockade of his headquarters, he meets with a group of international peace activists in Ramallah.

Palestinian Authority has formal control, in the disputed territories, and in Israel itself. Millions of Palestinians live in Jordan, and hundreds of thousands live in other countries of the Middle East. Many more have made their homes in Europe, the United States, and other countries of the world.

Palestinians are spread across the globe because they

do not have a country of their own. Much of the territory that Palestinians claim as theirs is also claimed by Israel. Some Palestinians claim all the territory occupied by Israel in a war that took place in 1948, but most claim only the right to the territory that Israel captured during another war in 1967. This dispute over territory has led to many wars and to devastating terrorist attacks carried out by Palestinians against Israeli citizens. The conflict continues to cause death and bloodshed.

Yasser Arafat has made it his life's work to attempt to establish a state for the Palestinian people. While Palestinians and their ancestors have lived in the region for centuries, they have never had a modern, independent state. This goal is the cause for which Arafat has studied, planned, suffered, fought, killed, and, on many occasions, nearly died. He has been both brilliant and foolhardy, patient as well as violent. He has mixed with kings and presidents, and he has shared his dinner table with people off the street. He has had lifelong friendships, but he has also made many enemies. It is not without good reason that he is spoken of as the "father of Palestine."

One of Arafat's closest friends and colleagues, Khalil Wazir, who was killed in 1988, said of Arafat, "He is not just our leader. He lives all of our fears, all of our dreams and all our sufferings. In one person he is all of us, all of our emotions, all of our strengths, all of our weaknesses, all of our contradictions."

As a child, Yasser Arafat played in streets much like this one in a Cairo, Egypt, neighborhood.

Chapter **TWO**

WATCHING AND LEARNING

YASSER ARAFAT'S FATHER, ABDEL RAOUF ARAFAT al-Qudwa al-Husseini, was a merchant trader. He made his living by trading goods—mostly textiles and foodstuffs. In the early 1900s, he lived with his wife, Zahwa Abu Saoud, in Gaza. Gaza is a small strip of land located in what was then Palestine, a region east of Egypt. At that time, Egypt was the richest country in the Arab world, and it attracted many people in search of a better life. Abdel Raouf Arafat, his wife, and their five children moved to Cairo, Egypt's capital, in 1927. Egypt was a center for trading and suited Arafat's business. He invested in a factory making processed cheese. The finished products were distributed throughout the Arab world, and business prospered.

BIRTH OF A SON

Mohammed Abdel Rahman Abdel Raouf Arafat al-
Qudwa al-Husseini—whom the world would later know
as Yasser Arafat—was born on August 24, 1929, in
Cairo. Like most Arabic names, Arafat's name breaks
down into several parts. For example, Mohammed is his
given name, Abdel Raouf is his father's name, Arafat is
his grandfather's name, and al-Husseini is the name of
his extended clan.

Mohammed was the family's sixth child, with three
older sisters—Inam, Khadija, and Yusar—and two older
brothers—Khalid and Mustapha. A younger brother,
named Fathi, was born after Mohammed. Mohammed
got along better with his mother, Zahwa, than he did
with his father. The elder Arafat demanded strict
discipline, from both his children and from himself. He
walked everywhere, to and from work and also to visit
customers and suppliers. He walked up to twenty miles
a day and displayed an impressive level of fitness. He
also showed a humanitarian streak, giving to the poor.

In 1933, when Mohammed was four years old,
disaster struck: Zahwa died of a kidney ailment.
Mohammed's father soon remarried, and none of the
children liked their stepmother. Some observers believe
the children's dislike was one reason that the marriage
ended in divorce after only a few months.

Abdel Raouf Arafat sent Mohammed and Fathi to
Jerusalem to live with their maternal uncle, Selim Abul
Saoud. Jerusalem—at that time a part of Palestine—is a

Muslims pray at the al-Aqsa Mosque in Jerusalem. Behind the mosque is the Dome of the Rock. These are two of the holiest sites in the Islamic religion.

holy city, with deep religious significance for Christians, Jews, and Muslims. The city contains places of worship for all three of these religions, with Christian churches, Jewish synagogues, and Muslim mosques. Arafat's uncle lived in the old part of the city very near the three foremost religious sites in the city: the Western Wall, the Dome of the Rock, and al-Aqsa Mosque. Mohammed had been raised as a Muslim in Cairo, and he spent these formative years in Jerusalem learning more about the religion of Islam.

In the 1930s, Palestine was not an independent country. It was ruled by Britain under a mandate assigned by the League of Nations. Most of Palestine's population were Arab Muslims, and many Palestinians protested British-supported Jewish immigration into Palestine. A conflict known to Palestinians as the Great Rebellion broke out in 1936. Palestinians used boycotts, terrorist attacks, and other tactics in an attempt to weaken British control and halt Jewish immigration.

WHERE AND WHAT IS PALESTINE?

alestine is often referred to as the Holy Land, and it is claimed by Christians, Muslims, and Jews as the cradle of each of their civilizations and cultures. The historical region lay between the Mediterranean Sea to the west and the Arabian Desert to the east. Inhabited by Jewish settlers in about 2000 B.C.E., over the centuries the area was ruled by the Egyptians, Philistines (from whom Palestine takes its name), Assyrians, Babylonians, Persians, and Greeks. It came under the Roman Empire's control in 63 B.C.E. The Romans destroyed Jewish temples and ejected the Jews from the region.

After the era of Roman rule ended, the region was controlled by the Byzantine Empire. Beginning in around C.E. 700, it was almost continuously ruled and mostly inhabited by Muslims, including a period of hundreds of years when it was part of the Turkish (Ottoman) Empire.

By the end of the 1800s, a Jewish group known as Zionists began to press for a Jewish state that would bring together the Jewish diaspora from around the world. The diaspora was made up of millions of Jews, the descendants of those who had been exiled from their homeland by the Romans. The Zionists' founder, Theodor Herzl, advocated the creation of the new Jewish state in Palestine because of the region's religious significance. The Zionist movement gathered strength, gaining support from Jews in many nations.

An international conflict called World War I broke out in 1914, and British troops were pitted against Turkish forces. Seeking military assistance, Britain promised independence to Arab lands under Ottoman rule in return for Arab support in the war. These lands included Palestine. But the British also promised to help establish a Jewish state. This promise was made in the famous Balfour Declaration of 1917, which was a short, informal letter to the Zionist leader Lord Rothschild. The letter read in full:

Dear Lord Rothschild

I have much pleasure in conveying to you on behalf of His Majesty's Government the following declaration of sympathy with Jewish Zionist aspirations which has been submitted to, and approved by the Cabinet.

His Majesty's Government view with favour the establishment in Palestine of a national home for the Jewish people, and will use their best endeavours to facilitate the achievement of this object, it being clearly understood that nothing shall be done which may prejudice the civil and religious rights of the existing non-Jewish communities in Palestine, or the rights and political status enjoyed by Jews in any other country.

I should be grateful if you would bring this declaration to the knowledge of the Zionist Federation.

Yours sincerely,
Arthur Balfour, British Secretary of State for Foreign Affairs

This letter was to have far-reaching effects. In late 1917, British troops entered Palestine under the terms of a mandate assigned to Britain by the international community. Britain started to permit significant emigration of Jews to Palestine. Residents of Palestine, most of whom were Arab Muslims, resented the influx. Even more Jewish immigrants arrived after World War II (1939–1945), during which millions of Jews were put to death in concentration camps by the German Nazis. After the horrors of this event—known as the Holocaust—many Jews sought a safe haven.

The British government found itself attacked, both politically and violently, by both Jews (for not permitting enough Jewish immigration) and Arabs (for allowing too much). In 1947 Britain asked the United Nations—an international body set up after World War II to promote world peace—to help resolve the problem. Despite many rounds of UN discussion, the Jewish and Arab sides of the conflict could not reach a compromise until after a war in 1948, which brought the creation of the state of Israel.

In response, British soldiers often used violent tactics to keep the Arab population under control and, sometimes, to temporarily curb Jewish immigration. One of Mohammed's earliest memories was of British soldiers breaking into his uncle's house late at night, while the family was asleep, and smashing furniture. Mohammed, like many other Palestinian children, vented his own frustration with the situation by throwing stones at British soldiers and slashing the tires of British vehicles.

In 1937, when Mohammed was eight years old, he and Fathi returned to Cairo for reasons that are not known. Their father had by then married for a third time, and his new wife was as unpopular with the children as his second wife had been. The young Mohammed was largely brought up by his older sister, Inam, but he soon learned to fend for himself. He was an energetic child and developed a rebellious streak. He often skipped school, taking to the streets and playing with other kids there. As a young boy, Mohammed liked to command other children, making them march and drill and beating them with a stick if they disobeyed an order.

Yet he also inherited some of his father's kindness. When Inam gave Mohammed a new suit, he said he would not wear it unless the poorer children with whom he played on the streets were also given new suits.

During World War II, the British used Egypt as a base from which to fight the Germans, and they kept a tight grip on the Suez Canal. This waterway, which had been cut through Egypt to create a passageway between the Mediterranean Sea and the Red Sea, was a fast and safe route for ships traveling between Europe and Asia. In the Arab world, many people opposed Britain's control of the canal. Revolutionary politics were in the air, especially among young students, and Mohammed absorbed the mood.

MAKING CONNECTIONS

In 1946 seventeen-year-old Mohammed met the mufti of Jerusalem, Haj Amin al-Husseini. The mufti, who was on a visit to Cairo at the time, was the most senior political and religious leader in Palestine. A distant relative of Mohammed, Sheikh Hassan Abu Saoud, was traveling with the mufti. Mohammed, as a fiery young man eager to make his mark in the world, asked if he could make himself useful. Mohammed became the sheikh's unofficial assistant, helping out with odd jobs such as spreading the elder's prayer mat, providing information about the activities of Palestinians in Egyptian schools and universities, and collecting money for the Palestinian fight for freedom from British rule.

In Palestine the campaign against the British and the growing conflict with Jewish immigrants were taking on an increasingly military dimension. For example, Mohammed became involved in a publicity stunt to try to convince the Egyptian government to supply arms to Palestinian activists. He and some friends bought an inexpensive, secondhand armored car from a scrap metal dealer and pushed it to the Foreign Ministry in Cairo, where it was draped with Palestinian flags. It is not known whether the government provided arms as a result of this stunt. However, the incident drew much attention from locals and the press and showed Mohammed how valuable such publicity could be in bringing the Palestinian cause to a wider audience.

As he became more involved in the Palestinian cause, Mohammed chose to give himself a cover name. Many people believe that this was when he began going by "Yasser" Arafat. In Arabic Yasser means "easygoing" or "carefree," which described one side of his character. The name also had historical associations. Ammar ibn Yasser was a celebrated Muslim warrior. He was also a companion of the prophet Muhammad, who founded the religion of Islam in the C.E. 600s. The historical Yasser was regarded as a symbol of patience and steadfastness, qualities which the newly named Yasser liked to think he also had.

UPHEAVALS IN PALESTINE

In 1947 Yasser enrolled in Cairo University, studying for a degree in civil engineering. Meanwhile, the postwar political situation in Palestine was becoming more unstable every day. The British had not been able to resolve the region's future to the satisfaction of both Jews and Arabs. The British were also becoming the target of terrorist attacks. The worst of these had been a bomb planted at the King David Hotel in Jerusalem in July 1946 by a radical Jewish group, Irgun Zwei Leumi, led by Menachem Begin. The hotel had been chosen for the attack because it was the British military and civilian headquarters.

In 1947 the British decided to end their mandate over the territory. The United Nations then proposed an arrangement called partition, under which the territory would be divided into two states: Israel, for the Jewish community, and Palestine, for the Palestinians. The plan was immediately accepted by Jews, who were delighted that their dream of a country of their own had been accepted by the international community. However, the plan was rejected by the Palestinian Arabs, who still claimed the whole territory as their own. Nothing came of the UN plan, which was summarized in a document called UN Resolution 181.

As British control drew to a close, renewed violence erupted between Palestinians (who were often aided by fighters from other Arab nations) and Israelis. The turmoil included riots, raids on Arab villages and Jewish settlements, and fighting in the streets. On April 8, 1948, Abdel Kader Husseini, a prominent Palestinian leader, was killed in skirmishes in Jerusalem. The British formally withdrew from Palestine, without having settled any boundaries between Palestinian and Israeli territories. On May 14, 1948, Israel declared a new state. Palestinians were enraged. The next day, the armies of five Arab countries (Egypt, Jordan, Lebanon,

Syria, and Iraq) launched an attack on Israel with the intention of annihilating the new state. The Arab attackers, however, underestimated Israel's capacity to fight. Not only did the Israeli armed forces repel the attacks, but they managed to capture territory which had been assigned to Palestinian Arabs by the UN partition plan. Hundreds of thousands of Palestinian Arabs fled to escape the fighting, many of them to the narrow Gaza Strip.

A truce was declared on June 11, followed by a formal cease-fire in 1949. After the fighting, Israel controlled three-quarters of the former territory of Palestine. Neighboring Arab countries took over control of the rest of the country. Jordan, to the east of Israel,

Arab soldiers fight Israeli troops at the gate to Jerusalem during the 1948 war between the newly declared state of Israel and Arab nations.

THE 1948 WAR

n the war of 1948, Palestinian militia, outside volunteers, and the partial armies of Egypt, Syria, Lebanon, Jordan, and Iraq faced off against Israeli forces. Reports vary widely on the number of fighters and the quality of weaponry on each side. Some state that the Israeli troops were vastly outnumbered, while others assert that the two sides were fairly evenly matched. At any rate, the Israeli troops soon proved much more capable than the Arab armies had expected.

Arab forces did achieve some victories. Jordan took control of the West Bank, an area of land stretching about twenty-five miles to the west of the Jordan River and extending about eighty miles from north to south. Egyptian and Palestinian forces retained control of the Gaza Strip, a small corner of land along the Mediterranean coast. Arafat himself fought in this area with units of the Muslim Brotherhood (a militant Islamic organization founded in Cairo in 1929). But the rest of Palestine as it had been under the British mandate was captured by Israeli forces, thus becoming part of Israel.

assumed control of the West Bank. Egypt, to the west of Israel, took the Gaza Strip.

For the Arab countries in general, and for the Palestinians in particular, the war was a complete humiliation. Not only had the Arab forces lost a decisive war, but Palestine had lost a chance at statehood. The war came to be known by Arabs as "the catastrophe."

N

LEBANON

SYRIA

Sea of Galilee

Nazareth

Mediterranean Sea

Jordan River

Amman

TRANSJORDAN
(later, Jordan)

Tel Aviv

Jerusalem

Gaza

Dead Sea

ISRAEL

EGYPT

Key

Allotted to Israel in UN plan

Allotted to Palestinians in UN plan and retained by Arab states (Egypt and Jordan)

Allotted to Palestinians in UN plan and seized by Israel in 1948 war

| 0 | 50 miles |
| 0 | 80 km |

SAUDI
ARABIA

This map shows the changing borders of Israel and the Palestinian territories.

NEW DIRECTIONS

The war of 1948 had a profound effect on Yasser Arafat. His political and military activities became far more important to him than his studies. He joined the Egyptian Union of Students and through this group made contact with other students who were enraged by what they saw as the humiliation suffered by Palestinians. Arafat set up basic military training camps on the campus of the University of Cairo. In 1949 he and some other students started a new magazine, the *Voice of Palestine*. The Palestinian students took their lead from a rebel movement in Egypt, the Free Officers' Movement (FOM), which was plotting to overthrow that country's king, Farouk. The leader of the FOM was a man called Gamal Abdel Nasser. The movement's plot eventually succeeded, and on July 23, 1952, King Farouk of Egypt was toppled in a military coup headed by Nasser.

Arafat soon displayed a talent for leadership and organization. He was energized and passionate. Each day he went to the university campus by train. The station was conveniently close to the Arafat family apartment. Not wishing to waste a single second waiting for the train on the platform, Arafat listened for the sound of the train while he was still at home. When he heard it approaching, he would tear out of the house, leap over the front gate (which was always locked), and just manage to catch the train before it left. He never relied on his watch.

Gamal Abdel Nasser led the FOM rebels in Egypt. He also served as a mentor for Arafat.

Arafat rose through the ranks to become president of the Union of Palestinian Students, a group of young Palestinian activists at the university, in 1952. In that position, Arafat started to acquire a higher public profile. He persuaded the League of Arab States—a group of Arab nations, organized to help them work together—to pay the university tuition fees of Palestinian refugee students who were finding it difficult to pay their bills. Arafat was also among those who presented a petition to the new Egyptian president, General Mohammed Naguib, asking him not to ignore the Palestinian situation. The petition was written in blood—to show that the Palestinian cause was as important to Arab students as the blood flowing through their veins.

While Arafat earned a reputation for his dedication and hard work, he also earned some enemies by displaying a violent temper and showing intolerance of others. He never grew close to his father, either. When his father died in 1952, Arafat did not go to his funeral.

By 1954 Arafat was working closely with an activist named Khalil Wazir. About six years younger than Arafat, Wazir had escaped Palestine with his family in 1948. Both Wazir and Arafat seethed at the situation, which had left Israel in control of what Wazir and Arafat considered to be the Palestinians' homeland.

The two agreed on a strategy of attacking sites that were essential to Israelis' lives and to the smooth running of the country. Water was in short supply in the region. By blowing up water pipes and supplies, Arafat and Wazir and their supporters made life very difficult for Israelis. They launched a number of raids from Gaza into Israel. The strategy was based on the idea of provoking Israel into retaliatory action so that the Palestinians would have a reason to fight another war. This time the Palestinians might win.

As he assumed a higher profile, Arafat started to anger some very influential people, who felt that he was showing too much independence. Nasser, by this time the most powerful person in Egypt, was wary of his young political admirer. When the Muslim Brotherhood attempted to assassinate Nasser in October 1954, Arafat was arrested because of his association with the group. Arafat denied he was a member of the brotherhood, but he was put in prison for two months.

As an Egyptian citizen by birth, Arafat had to do military service in Egypt. This service restricted his activities and was a distraction from his main focus of attention. However, he used the experience to learn about military matters, such as bomb disposal, that might be useful to the Palestinian campaign.

In July 1956, Arafat completed his university studies and graduated as a civil engineer. He soon created and chaired a group of Palestinian graduates. This organization allowed him to be politically active and to forge links with other like-minded Palestinians. He also used his academic qualifications to get a job as an engineer with an Egyptian construction company.

Nationalizing the Suez Canal

In August 1956, Arafat and Wazir traveled to Prague, Czechoslovakia, to attend an international students' congress. Arafat recognized that this trip was another chance to draw attention to the Palestinian cause. He decided to wear a kaffiyeh, a very distinctive headdress that was uncommon in Europe at the time. The kaffiyeh is a powerful Palestinian symbol. Palestinian fighters had worn the headdress during the Great Rebellion of 1936. The headdress drew attention to Arafat and raised awareness of his cause.

While Arafat and Wazir were in Prague, Nasser, who had become president of Egypt, took the dramatic step of claiming full Egyptian control and ownership of the Suez Canal. At the time, this strategically vital waterway was jointly controlled by Egypt, Britain, and France, and the move infuriated Britain and France. Joining forces with the Israeli government, which accused Egypt of supporting Palestinian fighters, they drew up a plan to recover the canal by force. Israel attacked Egypt on October 29, 1956, and soon took control of the Gaza Strip and most of the Sinai Peninsula, both part of Egyptian territory. But Egypt refused to back down, even when British and French forces went into action. The fighting stopped only when the United Nations intervened. The UN-brokered cease-fire required Israel to withdraw from the Gaza Strip and Sinai Peninsula. Egypt was allowed to keep control of the Suez Canal on the condition that it allow

British troops and equipment parachuted into Egypt during the Suez Canal crisis of 1956.

international traffic to pass through. To keep the peace, UN troops moved in to guard the Israeli-Egyptian border. In addition to maintaining the cease-fire between Israel and Egypt, these forces prevented Palestinian fighters from using Gaza to launch additional raids into Israel. This deterrent to their activities meant that it was time for a change of scene for Arafat and his colleagues.

Arafat, shown wearing the kaffiyeh. He grew in stature as Fatah, the organization he helped form to wage armed struggle against Israel, gained money and support from the Arab world.

Chapter **THREE**

THE MAKING
OF A
REVOLUTIONARY

IN **1957 ARAFAT LEFT EGYPT TO MAKE A NEW**
life for himself in the nearby nation of Kuwait. As a
qualified engineer, he found no difficulty in getting
work. He took a job with the Kuwait Public Works
Department and also did some other part-time work.
He earned a good living, and, provided with free living
quarters by his employer as a benefit of the job, he had
plenty of cash.

This period was probably the most relaxed and
comfortable existence that Arafat had ever enjoyed. He
had few worries. He was away from his family and able
to live a fully independent life. No longer involved in
direct combat, he did not have to fear for his own
safety. And yet, in some ways, Arafat lived simply. Not

interested in fancy meals, he barely bothered to cook for himself. He lived on a diet of cornflakes, toast, and tea with honey. For relaxation, he watched cartoons on television. *Tom and Jerry* was one of his favorites. He read little, relying more on late-night discussions with friends and colleagues, such as Khalil Wazir and Salah Khalaf (a friend from the Egyptian Union of Students who had also moved to Kuwait), to hone his political instincts.

Arafat loved cars and travel. With money no object, he acquired a number of cars, including a Thunderbird and a Volkswagen. Of the vehicles, his favorite was the open-topped Thunderbird. Wearing dark sunglasses and already losing his hair, Arafat was an eye-catching figure in his sports cars. He would sometimes drive all the way to Lebanon to shop. He also had time and money to take holidays. During his time in Kuwait, Arafat visited Europe on holiday, traveling to Greece, Italy, France, Switzerland, and Austria.

REVOLUTION IN THE AIR

But Arafat was not satisfied with a life of ease. Revolution was in the air in many parts of the world. In Vietnam and Algeria, national independence movements were waging violent campaigns against the colonial rule of France. Iraq was in turmoil as people rose against the monarchy there. In the Caribbean nation of Cuba, Communist revolutionaries led by Fidel Castro threatened to overthrow the oppressive government. From his home in Kuwait, Arafat longed for his own revolution, and he was sure that he had the perfect cause: to create an independent state of Palestine. He dreamed of becoming a Palestinian hero.

Wazir and Khalaf had moved to Kuwait to become teachers. The three friends plotted their next move, which was to create an organization dedicated to a free Palestine. They called this organization Fatah. Fatah was an acronym, comprising the first letters of the words (in reverse order) of its full name: Harakat al-Tahrir al-Watani al-Falastini, which, in English, means "Palestinian Liberation Movement." The word *fatah* also means "conquest" or "victory."

The leaders of Fatah also gave themselves assumed code names as a way to heighten their fighting status and as a measure of protection and disguise. Arafat became "Abu Amar," which means "builder," referring both to his profession in construction work and to his involvement in building the state of Palestine. Khalil Wazir became "Abu Jihad" and Salah Khalaf became "Abu Iyad."

Even though Fatah started as a partnership, Arafat quickly became its leader. He was naturally more outgoing than the others, was a gifted speaker, and was very successful in raising money. Fatah started a magazine, *Our Palestine*, to publicize the Palestinian situation. The magazine made constant reference to "the catastrophe" of the loss of Palestine in the war of 1948. "Our destiny is being shaped, but our voice is not

Yasser Arafat, left, with his longtime colleague and fellow Palestinian activist, Khalil Wazir (also known as Abu Jihad), right

heard," the editors wrote. "The voice of the Palestinian people will not be heard until the sons of Palestine stand together in one rank. Our fundamental desire is for the land which was ours."

Fatah's objective was nothing less than the capture of all the lands occupied by Israel. Arafat himself said, "The goal of our struggle is the end of Israel and there can be no compromise."

In July 1962, Arafat was honored when he, along with other foreign dignitaries, was invited by the Algerian government to attend a ceremony to celebrate the liberation of Algeria from the French. Arafat and his colleagues took heart from the achievement of the National Liberation Front in Algeria. After viewing the success of that liberation movement, they resolved that Palestinians should rely on themselves alone to mount a campaign against Israel and not become too dependent on outside Arab support.

In February 1963, Fatah set up a more formal organizational structure. Its leaders formed a central

NOT A ONE-MAN BAND

rafat is the best known of the Palestinian leaders, but he has rarely operated on his own. Others, too, have earned reputations for themselves in the Palestinian cause—though not always good ones.

The first prominent Palestinian leader was Abdel Kader Husseini. He died in battle on April 8, 1948.

Khaled al-Hassan (Abu Said), who fled Israel in 1948, arrived in Kuwait before Arafat and was a contributor to the publication *Our Palestine*. He became Arafat's principal rival.

Salah Khalaf (Abu Iyad) was one of Arafat's early acquaintances, but the two fell out when Khalaf took an openly violent approach to the struggle.

Khalil Wazir (Abu Jihad) was a good partner for Arafat. Wazir's cool head and deliberate manner contrasted with Arafat's hot-headedness and impetuousness.

George Habash, a medical doctor, earned a notorious reputation for initiating a policy of terrorism in the 1960s. Plane hijackings were the most dramatic of the tactics he adopted. He formed the Arab Nationalist Movement, which later became the Popular Front for the Liberation of Palestine (PFLP).

committee comprising ten people. This collective leadership meant that all major decisions had to be agreed upon by everyone on the committee.

The next step was to build up a fighting force. Training camps were set up in Algeria, Lebanon, and Syria, and the leadership moved to Syria as a group

Fatah commandos underwent basic military training. What Fatah members lacked in military skills, they tried to make up for in revolutionary spirit.

between 1963 and 1964. The decision to move was not easy. Arafat was living a good life in Kuwait and thought long and hard before giving it up. By signing up with the Palestinian revolution, he could never hope to enjoy such a life of ease again. Arafat parted with his beloved Thunderbird and his other sports cars, keeping only his battered old Volkswagen.

FRONT LINE

Syria was chosen as Fatah's headquarters for two reasons. The first reason was that Fatah had decided to embark on a course of attacks from territory adjoining Israel. Syria borders Israel, so its location would enable Fatah members to enter Israel fairly easily, launch their attacks, and then retreat to the relative safety of the neighboring country. The second reason was that a new pro-Palestinian leadership had seized power in Syria.

Arafat thought that he could rely on their support.

As they set up operations in Syria, Fatah could not keep regional politics and the Palestinian cause separate. Egypt and Syria both vied for the position as the leading Arab state in the Middle East, and each went to great lengths to upstage the other. When Syria lent its support to Fatah, Egypt moved to set up an alternative Palestinian group. In January 1964, the first Arab Summit Conference was held in Cairo. The leaders of the Arab countries agreed to a proposal by Egyptian president Nasser to create a new organization to promote the Palestinian cause. Called the Palestine Liberation Organization (PLO), the group named the fiery, unpredictable Ahmed Shukairy as its leader. Fatah, however, wanted nothing to do with the Palestine Liberation Organization. They suspected that

Ahmed Shukairy, center, was the first president of the Palestine Liberation Organization.

Shukairy would do only what Nasser told him to do.

Throughout the rest of 1964, Fatah prepared for what it hoped would be an effective series of raids into Israel. The training of fighters, who were called *fedayeen* (which means "men of sacrifice"), continued. So confident was Fatah that the raids would make a big impact that the organization released a statement on December 31, 1964, declaring that Fatah fedayeen had successfully destroyed Israeli property. Three days later, Fatah fighters did get over the border in an attempt to blow up a water diversion canal. However, the bomb didn't work properly and was discovered before it exploded.

Fatah's raids—some of them more successful than the first one—continued. At the same time, arguments over tactics and goals arose within the Fatah leadership, particularly between Arafat and Khaled al-Hassan (code name Abu Said). Another problem was that Syria, which had been more sympathetic than other Arab countries to Fatah, was turning against the movement. Syria's minister of defense, Hafez al-Assad, thought that Fatah and Arafat were becoming too powerful in Syria. He did not trust Arafat and planned an unsuccessful attempt to have him assassinated. Arafat would later claim that he had a "nose" for danger and could sense when his life was threatened.

In May 1966, al-Assad tried a different tactic to curb the power of Fatah. Arafat, Abu Jihad, and a number of other Palestinian activists were arrested on trumped-up

A convoy of Arab vehicles lies in ruins after bombings by Israeli jets during the Six-Day War in 1967.

murder charges. After being released, following a hunger strike by Arafat and the intervention of his colleagues in Fatah, Arafat slipped out of the country, disguised as a corporal in the Syrian army.

This was not the first time that Yasser Arafat adopted a disguise to escape his enemies. At various times during this period, as he traveled between Lebanon, Syria, Jordan, and the West Bank, he disguised himself as a Pakistani businessman, an Egyptian tourist, a shepherd, and even once as an old woman.

THE SIX-DAY WAR

Meanwhile, trouble was brewing once again between Egypt and Israel. President Nasser of Egypt was determined to avenge two previous Arab defeats in conflict with Israel. In May 1967, Nasser stationed two divisions of his army along Israel's border. This action was prompted by warnings delivered by Egypt's ally, the Soviet Union, that Israel was massing its army in preparation for an attack against Syria and Egypt. Nasser bragged publicly that if Israel attacked Syria or

Key

▨ Areas occupied by Israel in 1967

SYRIA

LEBANON
Beirut •

Mediterranean
Sea

• Damascus
Golan
Heights

Jerusalem
Gaza
Strip

• Amman

• Gaza
West
Bank

ISRAEL

JORDAN

Cairo •

Suez Canal

Sinai Peninsula
(returned to Egypt
between 1979
and 1982)

EGYPT

N

0   100 miles
0   160 km

SAUDI
ARABIA

Areas occupied by Israel during the Six-Day War in June 1967

Egypt, Egyptian forces would "destroy" Israel. This threat was enough to force Israel to act.

On June 5, Israel launched a series of attacks on its Arab neighbors, including Egypt. The Israeli armed forces were so well prepared that the Egyptian Air Force was destroyed on the ground before it had a chance to get airborne. In six days, Israel captured the Sinai Desert and the Gaza Strip from Egypt, the West Bank from Jordan, and the Golan Heights from Syria. Israel was also able to unify the two parts of Jerusalem (Jerusalem straddled the border between Israel and the West Bank). Called the Six-Day War, the conflict left Israel in control of an area of land that was four times the size of the territory it had controlled before the war.

Because the war was over so quickly, Arafat had no time to take part. In an attempt to do something useful, he and some of his Fatah colleagues filled his

Volkswagen with rocket-propelled grenades and headed for the Golan Heights in Syria. By the time they got there, the war was all but over.

The war was another enormous setback for the Palestinians. Before 1967 the people of Palestine could claim that Arab allies at least controlled the West Bank and Gaza, even if Palestine did not have a state of its own. After the Six-Day War, these stretches of territory were lost. Hundreds of thousands of Palestinian refugees fled the captured areas. The year of the war also brought a personal loss for Yasser Arafat. The house in which he had lived as a boy with his uncle in Jerusalem was knocked down to make way for new buildings.

Even in the face of such losses, Arafat refused to back down. He said, "I knew that if we did not act quickly the whole Arab nation, Arabs everywhere, would be infected by the psychology of defeat."

Palestinian refugees cross the Allenby Bridge into Jordan in August 1967, under the watch of Israeli soldiers policing the bridge.

Yasser Arafat was constantly on the move in the 1960s, especially after the end of the Six-Day War.

Chapter **FOUR**

FAME AND NOTORIETY

AFTER THE DEFEAT IN THE SIX-DAY WAR, FATAH was more determined than ever to continue the fight for the Palestinian cause. However, the Palestinians had neither a central army nor a territory in which to base it. The best that their fighters could hope for was to adopt a strategy of sabotage and terrorism, staging raids across the border to damage installations and make life difficult for Israeli citizens and security forces.

Another obstacle was the fact that Fatah had been expelled from both Egypt and Syria. Jordan was the next best choice as a base of operations. Jordan had a long border with Israel and, until the losses in the 1967 war, had been in occupation of the West Bank. Half of Jordan's population was Palestinian. Fatah moved its center of operations to the East Bank, which lies across the Jordan River from the West Bank.

After Jordan's loss of the West Bank, Arafat believed that it was vital to maintain direct links with Palestinians who remained in that area of the country. He paid several visits to the West Bank, always in disguise, to meet local people and to enlist support for Fatah. He even managed to set up a sort of headquarters in a village near Jenin. As he traveled through the area, he used various pseudonyms. He also earned the nickname "the old man," given to him by the local Palestinians.

Arafat became a sort of Palestinian secret agent, eluding the Israeli authorities, who wanted to prevent him from operating in Israeli territory. He slept very little. When he did rest, he almost never slept in the same house twice. He turned up unexpectedly in remote places, where he would quickly generate support among the locals and then disappear just as suddenly as he had come. Through these efforts, he was very successful in rallying support from many sections of the local population. One group with whom he came into contact was the Union of Palestinian Women. One of this group's members, Raymonda Tawil, was a prominent campaigner for the Palestinian cause. When a house in Ramallah in which Arafat was staying was surrounded by Israeli troops, the women helped him escape. He left just in the nick of time. According to an eyewitness, "The Israeli security forces encircled the villa and broke into it. They found a warm bed and boiling tea but Arafat was not there."

ARAB SUPPORT

At the same time that Fatah adopted a policy of self-reliance, it started to receive wholehearted support from Arab countries. In September 1967, the Arab Summit Conference in Khartoum, Sudan, gave its full backing to the Palestinian cause and to the policy of armed struggle. The Arab leaders committed themselves to a radical policy of three "noes:" no negotiations with Israel, no recognition of Israeli statehood, and no peace.

The international community also weighed in with a pronouncement on the Palestinian-Israeli conflict. At the United Nations, Resolution 242 was passed by a unanimous vote on November 22, 1967, requiring Israel to return territories captured during the Six-Day War to the countries from which the land had been seized. However, the resolution contained some unclear language and has been the subject of much argument ever since.

The resolution, for instance, made no direct mention of the Palestinians, other than referring to a "refugee problem." Palestinians, however, did not see themselves this way. Many hundreds of thousands of Palestinians were living as refugees in camps in Arab nations, but they believed they would one day return to their homes.

Meanwhile, the newly promised Arab support for Fatah spelled the end for Ahmed Shukairy's leadership

of the Palestine Liberation Organization. Shukairy had
been a very ineffective leader, and many people in the
region felt that Arafat was a more natural head of the
Palestinian movement. Shukairy was removed as the
PLO leader, and Fatah eventually merged with the PLO,
gaining an influential role in the organization.

Fatah's move to Jordan was finally completed in early
1968. Fatah hoped to launch a dramatic Palestinian
revolution. The Fatah fedayeen did not tell King
Hussein of Jordan their detailed plans. Israeli
intelligence, however, was aware of what the Fatah men
were doing. In particular, Israel knew that the main
camp used by the Palestinian fighters was at Karameh,
in the East Bank. The Israeli armed forces launched an
attack on the fedayeen there in March 1968. The odds
were heavily against the Palestinians, who were fewer
in number and not as well equipped as the Israeli
troops. However, the Palestinian fighters were
determined and well-organized, and they held off the
Israeli attack until the Jordanian army arrived to force
the Israelis to withdraw.

Arafat played a prominent role in the battle of
Karameh. While some people had urged Palestinian
fighters to retreat into nearby hills for their own safety,
Arafat ordered them to fight even when it became
known that Israel was going to attack. Arafat's decision
could have ended in disaster, but he skillfully
commanded the men in battle and displayed a firm
grasp of military tactics.

Karameh was Fatah's finest hour. High Palestinian losses during the battle meant that it could not be claimed as a complete victory. But Fatah's forces, with Jordanian help and weapons, had managed to repel the Israeli troops and inflict strong casualties. The propaganda value of the success was huge, and news of the battle spread through television and radio reports. Gifts, money, and clothing started arriving from Arab nations. At about the same time, the PLO published the Palestinian National Covenant, a statement outlining their ideas for setting up a state of Palestine.

LEADER OF THE PALESTINIANS

Arafat's rise to fame, however, upset others in the Palestinian movement, who felt that he was claiming too much of the glory for himself and who disagreed with his strategy. They felt that a policy of hit-and-run attacks did not inflict any significant damage on Israel. They argued for a strategy that would inflict more damage and casualties.

One person, in particular, took an opposing stance to Arafat. His name was George Habash. Habash favored a much more violent and radical approach to the Palestinian situation. He formed a group called the Popular Front for the Liberation of Palestine (PFLP). The violent policy adopted by the PFLP involved hijacking airplanes. The first PFLP hijacking was of an El Al (Israel's national airline) aircraft in July 1968. The hijackers successfully demanded the release of

George Habash, left, was the guerrilla leader of the Popular Front for the Liberation of Palestine (PFLP). The PFLP carried out terrorist attacks against Israelis in the late 1960s and early 1970s.

Palestinian fighters who had been captured by Israeli forces. Encouraged by this success, the PFLP planned more attacks for the future.

But despite the PFLP's opposition to his control, Karameh was still a legendary achievement for Arafat. His face became well known around the world. He took to wearing his kaffiyeh all the time, which he folded to resemble the shape of Palestine's historical borders—or, some people said, to look like a dagger. He wore dark glasses and military fatigues and carried a stick, which he held to look like a field marshal's baton. Around his neck, he wore a pendant containing a proverb from the Quran (the holy book of Islam). He even appeared on the cover of *Time* magazine in December 1968.

Despite his growing fame, Arafat continued to live quite modestly. In Jordan's capital city of Amman, he lived in an apartment with other Fatah leaders. He cooked and ate with his bodyguards, preferring to eat with other people rather than on his own. For his guests, this habit was something of a mixed blessing, because Arafat liked very bland food, often little more than vegetable soup. For dessert, he liked to eat Arab sweets made from honey and sesame seeds. To stay fit, he exercised regularly. His only relaxing pastimes were reading comics, watching cartoons, and spending time playing Ping-Pong.

After many years of foiling attempted assassinations, Arafat almost caused his own death in January 1969. A notoriously bad driver, he was involved in a terrible car crash, when his car ended up underneath a truck that had been coming toward him. But once again he survived, sustaining only minor injuries.

Arafat made the cover of Time *magazine on December 13, 1968, after the battle of Karameh. The publication brought the Palestinian leader to the attention of a worldwide readership.*

MOUNTING TENSIONS

The following month, Arafat was elected leader of the PLO. The PLO issued a document called the Charter of the Palestine Liberation Organization, committing its members to armed struggle for the "total liberation" of the Palestinian people.

The charter also stipulated the formation of the Palestine National Council (PNC), which was intended to be the PLO's supreme governing body. The PNC was scheduled to meet once a year. It was made up of representatives from the Palestinian guerrilla

Yasser Arafat, left, newly elected as leader of the PLO, meets in Cairo with Gamal Abdel Nasser, right, then Egypt's president, in 1969.

organizations, other Palestinian institutions, and from the Palestinian diaspora in the Arab world. Though not separate from the PLO, the PNC was in a position to approve or disapprove of PLO activities.

Upon becoming the PLO's leader, Arafat declared that his followers were committed to the Palestinian cause and were prepared to fight for it because they believed in democracy and had the freedom to say yes or no to the idea of resistance and struggle. Although many observers believed that Arafat's new leadership was less of a democracy than a dictatorship, it was clear that the PLO would indeed fight. Battle lines were drawn, as Arafat and the PLO continued to plan and execute strikes against Israel.

Though most Arab leaders publicly claimed a commitment to the destruction of Israel, many of them were privately less wedded to this position. Seeking assistance to defuse Arab-Israeli tensions, King Hussein of Jordan and President Nasser of Egypt approached the United States. The reaction in Washington was mixed. Henry Kissinger, President Richard Nixon's national security advisor, was opposed to what he thought might be rushed negotiations. At the same time, Secretary of State William Rogers was hoping that Egypt and Jordan might each make their own separate peace with Israel, possibly motivated by ambitions to reclaim captured territory. However, the PLO, Syria, and Israel all strongly opposed the effort for compromise, and in the end, nothing came of Hussein's and Nasser's initiative.

THE RISE OF TERRORISM

By that time, the PLO's actions, combined with the presence of so many Palestinians on Jordanian soil, were leading to serious friction. Arafat had fallen out with King Hussein, and the PLO had publicly called for protests and strikes against the Jordanian government. Jordanian armed forces and police engaged in skirmishes with Palestinian fighters. The region teetered on the edge of war.

Then, on September 6, 1970, any hopes of defusing the situation were shattered when the PFLP successfully hijacked four airliners and blew up three of them in Jordan after evacuating the passengers. The scale and coordination of this attack were unprecedented and brought the existence of the Palestinians to the attention of the world. It is not clear how much Arafat knew of the attack or whether he approved of it. Some historians believe that he secretly supported this atrocity even if he had taken no part in it.

The PFLP's choice of Jordan as the site for the destruction of the hijacked planes was the last straw for Hussein, who ordered attacks on PLO headquarters and Palestinian camps in Jordan. The violence escalated rapidly into a civil war. The conflict drew international attention, and other countries soon became involved, with Syria assisting the Palestinians, and Israel and the United States backing Jordan. In the end, Egypt's president Nasser was called in to mediate. Nasser

Yasser Arafat, center, *in Ramtha, Jordan, in October 1970. At the time, Arafat feared that his enemies in Jordan were trying to assassinate him.*

managed to arrange a cease-fire. Just hours later, Nasser died of a heart attack.

After the war, called Black September by Palestinians, Arafat once again had assassins on his trail. Members of the Jordanian army broke into Arafat's house, only to discover that he had left the building just moments before, somehow evading their clutches. Then the authorities in Jordan tried to prevent him from leaving the country. Arafat managed to escape once again. He had the help of a visiting royal from Kuwait, who lent Arafat his robes. Disguised as a sheikh, Arafat traveled to Amman airport and flew to Lebanon.

These assassination attempts and the turmoil that followed the fighting between Jordan and the Palestinian guerrillas led Arafat to fear for his life. In April 1971, Arafat traveled to Syria, but he found that

BLACK SEPTEMBER

The Black September Organization had emerged in September 1971 as a response to the September 1970 war in Jordan. Operating as a violent terrorist faction that would appear to be independent, Black September actually acted on the behalf of the PLO and Arafat's Fatah. Black September operatives carried out vicious attacks against Jordanian and Israeli targets. Their first major act had been the assassination of Jordan's prime minister, Wasfi Tal, on November 28, 1971, in Cairo. But the atrocity at the Olympic Games in Munich was the event that brought Black September to the attention of the world. The news generated by the attack reinforced the belief of many Palestinians—including Arafat—that publicity was of the utmost value to the Palestinian cause.

In 1972 Black September took hostage and killed eleven Israeli athletes at the Munich Olympics. This photo shows one of the terrorists on a balcony outside the room where the athletes were held.

he was not safe there, either. Eventually Arafat settled in Beirut, Lebanon's capital, and continued his work for Palestine from there.

Meanwhile, although most of the fighting in Jordan had ended, the violence was far from over. A new Palestinian terrorist group, called Black September, appeared on the global stage with an agenda of revenge for the war.

Black September made its most shocking attack in September 1972. That month the Olympic Games were being held in Munich, West Germany. On September 5, gunmen first took hostage and then killed eleven Israeli athletes. The world was stunned.

Even as terrorist factions grew more brutal, other groups within Palestinian society yearned for an end to the violence. Although many Palestinians had fled during the wars of 1948 and 1967, more than one million still lived in the West Bank and Gaza. These people were growing more and more weary of the conflict. Most people simply wanted to live in peace. Groups within the Palestinian movement began wondering if they should recognize the existence of an Israeli state and accept the idea of Israelis and Palestinians living side by side. However, many Palestinians feared that neither Israel nor Arafat and the PLO would ever be willing to negotiate an agreement. The Israeli government did not recognize the PLO as a legitimate representative of the Palestinians, viewing it as a terrorist organization. Within the PLO, many people were still just as opposed to recognizing Israel. An end to the conflict was nowhere in sight.

A confident Yasser Arafat gives a news conference in Beirut,
Lebanon, in 1976.

Chapter **FIVE**

APPEARING ON THE WORLD STAGE

THE WORLD'S FEARS OF WAR IN THE MIDDLE EAST were soon confirmed. On October 6, 1973, the Jewish holy day of Yom Kippur, Egypt and Syria attacked Israel. The Arab nations hoped to recapture territory that they had lost to Israel in the 1967 war. Egypt's president, Anwar el-Sadat, thought that by starting the war on the most important Jewish holiday he would surprise Israel. At first, Sadat's plan seemed to work. The Arab armies drove deep into Israeli territory and inflicted heavy casualties. But the tide soon turned. Once Israel had recovered from the surprise of the attack, its armed forces sprang into action and swiftly forced back the Egyptian and Syrian armies. The Israeli army, which already controlled the Golan Heights

Israeli tanks prepare to advance into Syria during the Yom Kippur War of 1973.

adjoining Syria, pressed deeper into Syrian territory. In Egypt, Israeli troops crossed to the western bank of the Suez Canal and threatened to march into Cairo. On October 22, UN Resolution 338 called for a cease-fire.

The war had lasted eighteen days. Once again, the Arab side had fared worse than the Israeli side. For Arafat and the Palestinian movement, the Yom Kippur

War seemed like yet another blow to their hopes for a Palestinian state.

THE OIL WEAPON

Despite the military setback, the Arab world soon found another highly effective weapon to use for its cause. Much of the world's oil is buried beneath Middle Eastern deserts. By the 1970s, Europe and the United States relied heavily on the Arab countries in the region for their supplies of oil. Many of these oil-consuming countries were strong supporters of Israel. In October 1973, Arab oil-producing nations announced that they would stop selling oil to the United States and other nations that backed Israel.

The effect was instant and dramatic. Oil prices skyrocketed in the United States and Europe, and industries faced crippling energy shortages. In Britain, for example, the government was forced to introduce a three-day workweek so that oil and gas supplies would not run out. As the focus of international attention, the Arab world used the opportunity to highlight the cause of the Palestinians.

Arab pressure on the United States and Europe, combined with a UN resolution calling for a settlement of the oil conflict, resulted in peace talks in December 1973. The talks, held in Geneva, Switzerland, were attended by representatives of Israel, Egypt, Jordan, the United States, and the Soviet Union. Arafat and the PLO were not invited.

In early January, the meetings ended without much progress. However, later that month, Israel and Egypt signed an agreement that resulted in the withdrawal of Israeli troops from several miles of the Sinai Peninsula. Egyptian forces reoccupied the western bank of the Suez Canal and a small, adjoining strip of land in the Sinai. In addition, a UN buffer zone was established, with a neutral army stationed between the two warring sides. A similar agreement between Israel and Syria was achieved in May 1974.

The PLO was, at the same time, reassessing its position. Having lost another war against the powerful Israeli army, some Palestinian leaders felt that the policy of armed struggle should be reevaluated. Some leaders were also uncertain about the chances of ever winning control of all of the territory that the Palestinians hoped to possess. The PLO formulated a new approach, focused on diplomacy. The PLO's central council also accepted the idea of regaining only part of the originally claimed lands and called for the establishment of a national authority on any areas that did eventually return to Palestinian control.

While Israel and the United States were reluctant to negotiate with the PLO, its status continued to rise within the Arab world. In October 1974, at an Arab Summit Conference at Rabat, Morocco, the leaders of the Arab world agreed that the PLO was the sole legitimate representative of the Palestinian people. Israel and other nations objected to this definition, seeing the PLO as a terrorist organization and not a legitimate political group or government.

The Arab leaders at the summit also passed another significant resolution, which committed King Hussein of Jordan to hand back the West Bank to the Palestinians if and when the territory was liberated. Egypt was also committed to allowing the Palestinians control of the Gaza Strip, if and when that territory could be recovered from Israel. After the conference, Arafat was thrilled, saying, "This summit conference has been like a wedding feast for the Palestinians."

In addition to gaining regional support, Arafat was also winning broader support, which culminated in an invitation to address the United Nations General Assembly on November 13, 1974. He was delighted to be invited to address such a distinguished group. The assembly represented almost every country in the world, and Arafat hoped that his appearance would be an opportunity to argue the Palestinian case in front of the international community. But first he had to get there—which was not simple. The United Nations is based in New York City, and the U.S. government controls who enters the country by issuing visas. There was no guarantee that the United States would issue a visa to Arafat, whom many people viewed as a terrorist.

Traveling was always a risk for Arafat, and he knew that his enemies might use the opportunity of such a high-profile journey to New York to target him. While in the Middle East, he usually chose to travel by car, but for this trip to the United States, flying was the only option. Arafat knew that it was possible that someone would try to shoot down the plane. The Egyptian government made an aircraft available for his personal use. The Syrian government offered to charter a plane for him, too. But Arafat chose, finally, to fly in an aircraft chartered by the Algerian government, departing from Algiers.

Once in New York City, the risks to Arafat were still very high. The security arrangements for his visit were on a scale that the United Nations had never seen before. The whole complex was sealed off from the public for the weekend before his arrival. Tens of thousands of people gathered in the Hammarskjöld Plaza in front of the UN building to protest Arafat's invitation and to hear Israeli speakers argue their cases. Leading U.S. politicians, the New York mayor, and other prominent figures were present.

Arafat and his colleagues had prepared his speech very carefully, considering both what he would say and his appearance. When Arafat stood before the General Assembly, he was well-shaven and dressed in pressed military fatigues. Reports vary on whether or not he carried a gun. As usual, he wore his kaffiyeh. It was a dramatic occasion. Arafat closed his speech with words that became famous. "Today," said Arafat, "I have come bearing an olive branch [a symbol of peace] and a freedom fighter's gun. Do not let the olive branch fall from my hand."

Yasser Arafat speaks to the United Nations General Assembly in New York City on November 13, 1974.

The PLO won further triumphs at that UN meeting. The United Nations granted the PLO observer status, which is a form of international recognition allowing a group to take part in UN proceedings as an observer. UN Resolution 3236 was passed, recognizing the right of the Palestinians to self-determination—to decide

THE ARAFAT IMAGE

ith his appearance at the United Nations, Yasser Arafat found himself in the international spotlight more than ever. Yet, while he tried to project the image of a man who cared for nothing but his cause, he also had a streak of vanity. For example, he wore lifts in his shoes to make him appear taller than his height of five feet four inches. He distributed photos of himself sleeping on airplanes, rather than in a comfortable bed, to convey the idea that the Palestinian fight was more important than his personal comfort and that he was relentless in his efforts as an international statesman.

Arafat's new-found international prominence also led him to assert greater control over the PLO. He controlled funds and publicity. The Palestinian news agency, Wafa, published only what Arafat approved.

Yet even with the trappings of power, Arafat did not indulge himself. He did not smoke or drink. He ate simple food, as he had always done. He tried, when time allowed, to keep fit.

Arafat during his speech to the United Nations in 1974

their own status. The resolution also reaffirmed the right of Palestinian refugees to return to their homes. But Israel still did not recognize the PLO as an official authority. Israeli leaders wanted peace, but they vowed that terrorism would never succeed in winning a Palestinian state. The PLO found itself in a unique position. Palestine had become a state in exile, with its own government but without its own territory. Nevertheless, the PLO had achieved international recognition, and with that recognition came a steady and large source of funds, mostly from rich Arab states.

TROUBLE IN LEBANON

Meanwhile, trouble was brewing in Lebanon. Christians, Sunni Muslims, and Shiite Muslims (Sunni and Shiite Muslims are the two main sects of Islam) all live in Lebanon. During the 1970s, conflicts arose between Lebanese Christian and Muslim communities. In addition, the country had been home to a huge number of Palestinians in refugee camps ever since the war of 1948. Palestinian fighters and PLO members in these camps launched attacks on Israel, subjecting the camps to attack by Israeli troops in retaliation. Eventually, just as had happened in Jordan a few years earlier, the presence of Palestinian fighters on Lebanese soil heightened the tensions and conflicts that already existed.

By 1975 the turmoil in Lebanon had escalated into civil war between Lebanese Christians and Muslims.

The Palestinians (most of whom were Muslims themselves) allied themselves with Muslim groups, especially following Christian attacks on Palestinian refugee camps in Lebanon. Syria, which was sympathetic to the Muslim side, was also drawn into the conflict. Looking for help, Lebanese Christian forces turned to Israel for military assistance. Israel, which also felt threatened by Muslim interests, began sending aid to the Lebanese Christians in 1976.

While Arafat's fighters assisted Muslim forces in the war, Arafat himself sometimes found it difficult to reach them. When he traveled outside of Lebanon, it was almost impossible for him to get back into the country. On one occasion, he was only able to sneak across Lebanese borders aboard an Egyptian ship that was delivering corn.

As the conflict wore on, Arafat lost favor with Syrian leaders who wanted to defuse the growing crisis—in particular with Hafez al-Assad, who had become Syria's president. But the Lebanese fight was important to Arafat. The PLO was not supposed to operate in Jordan or Egypt. If Lebanon came under the control of the Israeli-supported Christian forces, it would likely be off-limits to the PLO as well. Arafat and the PLO were losing friends fast, and they needed Lebanon as an ally.

In the autumn of 1976, regional leaders, including Arafat, held an emergency Arab Summit Conference and agreed to a cease-fire in Lebanon. As the turmoil waned, changes also took place elsewhere in the world.

Syrian president Hafez al-Assad, left, meets U.S. president Jimmy Carter, right, assisted by an interpreter, center, in Geneva, Switzerland, in September 1977.

A change of presidency in the United States in November 1976 offered renewed hope for peace between Palestinians and Israelis. President Jimmy Carter was more willing than his predecessors had been to try to accommodate the Palestinians in the peace process. Carter held many talks with Middle Eastern leaders in the hopes of negotiating a lasting peace, meeting with Egyptian president Sadat, Syrian president al-Assad, and others.

In October 1977, the United States and the Soviet Union issued a joint declaration calling for new peace talks between the Arab states and Israel. These talks would further discuss the ideas that had been laid out in Resolution 242 ten years earlier. However, the talks never took place. It seemed that the drive toward peace had stalled again.

SADAT MAKES PEACE

While attempts at restarting the peace process foundered, Egypt's president Sadat decided to approach Israel directly. In November 1977, without prior discussion with his colleagues in the Arab world, he announced to the Egyptian parliament that he would travel to Israel—into the very heart of the "enemy"— and declare that Egypt wanted peace with its neighbor. Arafat was present in the Egyptian parliament—having been invited especially by Sadat—to hear this historic announcement. Arafat was furious. He felt that he had been tricked by Sadat into attending the parliament session that day so that the outside world would believe that the PLO supported Sadat's proposal. On the contrary, Arafat was firmly opposed to the idea. As he saw it, one of the Palestinians' greatest strengths was Arab unity. If the Arab world divided over the issue of

Israel, then Israel would have even less reason to compromise with the PLO.

Arafat left the Egyptian capital in a rage. But Arafat's anger did not stop Sadat from pressing ahead with his plans. After receiving an official invitation from Israeli prime minister Menachem Begin, Sadat traveled to Israel in late 1977. As the first Arab leader to openly

Arafat, center, flanked by Egyptian vice president Hosni Mubarak, left, and Mamdouh Salem, right, an Egyptian politician, at the 1977 session of the Egyptian parliament at which Egyptian president Sadat announced that he was going to visit Israel on a peace mission

recognize Israel and call an end to the violence, Sadat received a warm welcome. He addressed the Israeli parliament (the Knesset) to confirm that Egypt was willing to make peace directly with Israel, but he added that a resolution of the Palestinian situation would be necessary for a lasting peace. Following Sadat's address, negotiations sponsored by the United States took place. Israel agreed to return the Sinai Peninsula to Egypt, and in September 1978, the two nations signed a peace treaty at Camp David, the U.S. president's official country retreat. A second, more formal agreement was signed in March 1979. But Sadat would pay for his vision. In October 1981, he was assassinated by Islamic extremists, in part because of his efforts to reach a lasting peace with Israel.

Meanwhile, conflict continued to rage in the region. Ongoing Palestinian terrorist attacks on Israeli civilians, launched from PLO bases in Lebanon, had already prompted Israeli retaliation—including the bombing of PLO facilities and Palestinian refugee camps in Lebanon—on multiple occasions. After the peace accords, Arafat feared that, with Israeli troops no longer concerned with a potential attack from Egypt, Israel could concentrate on the turmoil in Lebanon. His fears were soon confirmed. Israeli forces invaded southern Lebanon in 1982 and reached as far as the southern suburbs of Beirut. By June 1982, Israeli troops had surrounded the city.

Arafat himself was a target in the conflict. He had

become used to evading capture, but this time Israeli fighter planes, using sophisticated technology, were aiming at him personally. To avoid them, Arafat was always on the move. He slept in the backs of his cars, in different houses, and even on the beach. He spread rumors to throw his pursuers off his trail. Yet despite all

Yasser Arafat, center, and aides examine a map of Beirut during the Israeli invasion of Lebanon in 1982.

this secrecy, Arafat felt that it was important to maintain appearances. He always made sure that his kaffiyeh was neatly pressed and that his shoes were polished.

Arafat talks to journalists before leaving the besieged city of Beirut for Tunis, Tunisia, on August 30, 1982.

The Palestinian fighters in Lebanon were brave but poorly trained and badly organized. It became clear that they could never hope to defeat the highly disciplined and well-equipped Israeli armed forces. Arafat saw that the time had come to back down. After mediation by the United States, it was agreed that the PLO fighters would be allowed a safe passage out of Lebanon and that Palestinian civilians in Lebanon would also be safe. Preparations for their departure began in July 1982, and Arafat himself was among the last to leave the following month, on August 30, 1982. He sailed away on the ship *Atlantis*, defiantly holding his hand in the victory sign. His final destination was Tunis, Tunisia. Thousands of PLO fighters were dispersed to nine different Arab countries.

The PLO no longer had a base in territory adjoining Israel, having been expelled from Jordan, Syria, and finally Lebanon. As part of the peace treaty with Israel, Egypt had agreed not to let Palestinian groups operate from its territory, either. Another phase of Arafat's life had come to an end.

Arafat makes a victory sign at the specially arranged session of the United Nations General Assembly in Geneva in December 1988—Arafat's second appearance before the United Nations.

Chapter **SIX**

ON THE ROAD TO NOWHERE

WITH ARAFAT AND THE FEDAYEEN REMOVED FROM Lebanon, the Israelis and the Christian militias in Lebanon had more control. But in September 1982, Bashir Gemayel, the Christian president-elect of Lebanon, was assassinated by a remote-controlled bomb. Two days later, Christian militias entered two of the largest Palestinian refugee camps, at Sabra and Shatila. The Lebanese forces claimed to be seeking PLO terrorists for capture, and Israeli troops, which still had control of the area, knew of the militias' entrance into the camps. But instead of arresting PLO members— who may not have even been in the camps—the Lebanese militias took revenge for Gemayel's death, massacring hundreds of Palestinian civilians.

After the attacks on the refugee camps, the PLO set up new headquarters in Tunis, out of the region and increasingly out of the picture. At the same time, Palestinian groups began directing their fighting against one another. The groups divided into pro-Arafat forces and anti-Arafat forces, the latter supported and encouraged by Syria.

Meanwhile, Arafat grew increasingly frustrated by what he saw as Israel's unwillingness to deal with him. While Israeli leaders viewed him as a ruthless terrorist, Arafat himself believed that he was the only person on the Palestinian side who could deliver a compromise that would lead to peace. Israel, he claimed, would regret it if he were no longer around.

Yasser Arafat, right, and PLO colleagues Khalil Wazir, center, and Abdul Rachman, left, visit the Lebanese port city of Tripoli in November 1983. Negotiations were under way for the withdrawal of Palestinian fighters from the city.

In September 1983, Arafat returned to Lebanon, where several thousand Palestinians who had remained in Lebanon after the PLO's departure were engaged in the new conflict. But by December, the tide had turned against Arafat and his followers again. They sailed from Lebanon to Egypt, protected by a French fleet.

Arafat's choice of destination was unexpected. Egypt was still shunned by most of the Arab world for its negotiations with Israel. But Arafat was losing friends. Most people viewed the infighting among Palestinian guerrillas with exasperation, and Arafat's enemies were pleased that the Palestinian movement was turning against itself. When necessary, Arafat could be very practical. He was always prepared to deal with anyone who could serve the Palestinian cause. So Arafat made peace with Egypt's new president, Hosni Mubarak.

Arafat also set about repairing his relationship with King Hussein of Jordan, which had been rocky. He and Hussein signed an accord in February 1985 and came up with a new strategy to try to advance the Palestinians' cause. They proposed the idea of a Palestinian state on the West Bank and the Gaza Strip. This state would be part of a joint Palestinian-Jordanian confederation. Jordanian leaders hoped that this approach, rather than a Palestinian state alone, might stand a better chance of winning approval from Israel. The United States gave tentative support to the joint initiative, even though the U.S. government was still opposed to dealing directly with the PLO.

While in Jordan, Arafat met Suha Tawil, a young Palestinian woman with whom he became friends. It was probably not the first time that they had met, since she was the daughter of the renowned Palestinian activist, Raymonda Tawil, who had led protests against the Israeli occupation during the 1960s and 1970s and with whom Arafat had come into regular contact.

ATTACK ON PLO HEADQUARTERS

Hopes of success for the joint Jordanian-Palestinian proposal received an immediate setback. On October 1, 1985, Israeli jets flew to Tunis and bombed the PLO headquarters. Israeli commanders may have assumed that Arafat would be inside. Arafat's extraordinary luck held again. He was out of the building, but the attack killed and injured dozens of people, including civilians and members of Arafat's staff.

That attack earned Arafat international sympathy. One week later, the hijacking of the Italian cruise liner the *Achille Lauro* and the killing of an American Jewish passenger by the hijackers had exactly the opposite effect. No one is certain whether or not Arafat knew about the hijacking before it happened. While Arafat had founded and led Fatah, the largest Palestinian guerrilla group, other PLO guerrilla groups operated under their own leaders, many of whom were more militant than Arafat. Although these groups were part of the PLO, led by Arafat, they did not necessarily accept Arafat's authority. But as the most prominent

Palestinian leader, Arafat was widely believed to be at least partially responsible for the hijacking.

Even before the *Achille Lauro* attack, the label "terrorist" had been applied to Arafat. Many Palestinian groups had been carrying out vicious acts of terror against Israelis—primarily civilians—since 1968. Hijackings, attacks on Jewish settlements and synagogues, and other terrorist activities had killed dozens of Israelis during Arafat's leadership of the PLO. Many people believed that he was fully supportive of these violent deeds. In November 1985, in what became known as the Cairo Declaration, he declared that he denounced "all forms of terrorism." However, the announcement carried little weight, as it specifically did not denounce armed struggle. King Hussein did not share Arafat's belief that armed struggle was a legitimate approach to the Palestinian situation, and the king announced early in 1986 that he was dropping the PLO as a partner for any peace negotiations.

THE BEGINNING OF THE INTIFADA

Up to this point, most Palestinian activism had been organized from outside Israel. However, many Palestinians still lived in the territories claimed by Israel. Their dissatisfaction with the situation was growing. December 1987 brought a new and unexpected development: the start of a Palestinian uprising called the intifada (literally meaning "shaking"). Violent protests took place within Israel,

Palestinian youths hurl stones at Israeli soldiers during the first intifada, a Palestinian uprising that began in December 1987.

largely carried out by young Palestinians living there.

The trigger for the protests was a relatively minor event. Four young Palestinians had been killed in a road accident in the Gaza Strip. In the refugee camp where the youths had lived, rumors spread that the accident had been deliberately caused by an Israeli. Anger and grief swept through the community. Protests and stone-throwing broke out at the funerals for the four men. Israeli soldiers on patrol shot one protester dead, and the violence exploded into even wider protests, which took the Israeli authorities by surprise and generated huge publicity. Pictures of young men, with their heads wrapped in kaffiyehs (which had become the main symbol of all Palestinians) throwing stones at Israeli tanks, made for dramatic headline images. The Palestinian historian Yezid Sayigh said that the intifada did more for the Palestinian cause in the space of a few weeks than years of armed struggle had been able to do.

Part of the reason for the outbreak of violence lay in the deep resentment felt by the Palestinian community, particularly over the issue of Israel's settlement policy after the Six-Day War. The Israeli government had begun erecting new homes for thousands of Jewish settlers in formerly Palestinian areas. Palestinians feared that this practice would make it very difficult for them to claim that land in the future. In addition, Palestinians' actions were restricted in territory held by Israel. Palestinians in these areas faced curfews, potential deportation, and other challenges such as press censorship and the closing of schools for Palestinian children. Most Palestinians felt as though they were second-class citizens. In addition, young Palestinians were becoming more and more frustrated at the lack of progress toward the establishment of a Palestinian state and at the ineffectiveness and corruption of the Palestinian leadership.

Arafat soon threw his support behind the intifada. He backed the establishment of a new group to organize and lead the intifada. Called the United National Leadership of the Uprising (UNLU), the group's membership was small and mostly secret. Members communicated with Palestinians inside Israel via transmitters and miniature receivers. Israel responded to the increasing organization of the uprising by sending a hit squad to assassinate Khalil Wazir, who was also rumored to be involved with the UNLU. Wazir was assassinated at his home in Tunis in April 1988.

SPLINTERING

With the intifada, the cohesiveness of the Palestinian movement splintered even more, as groups differed in outlook. The youth in the territories claimed by Israel were frustrated by the lack of progress. Other members of the movement felt that the core conflict was not over territory, but rather over religion—pitting Muslims against Jews—and they felt that the religious issues were just as important as the territorial issues. Radical Islamic movements, such as Hamas and Islamic Jihad, emerged to challenge the leadership of Arafat and the PLO and to commit acts of terrorism against Israelis.

Not for the first time, the region threatened to go up in flames. And not for the first time, this threat drew the United States to step in to try to find a solution. U.S. secretary of state George Shultz visited the region several times, calling for peace talks. However, in the eyes of many members of the U.S. government, there was still no legitimate reason to negotiate with the PLO.

Based in Tunis, Arafat had difficulty communicating with his contacts outside the country. He used the phone and fax machine a great deal and continued to receive a regular stream of visitors. One of them was Suha Tawil, whom he had last met in Jordan. Suha was able to travel to Tunis easily, usually coming from Paris, where her father, a wealthy banker, owned property. Her mother, Raymonda, was still heavily involved in efforts inside Israel to win support for peace with the Palestinians. She had also established contacts with Israelis who sought compromise with the Palestinians. Raymonda needed to report about these meetings to Arafat. Using Suha as a messenger was a very convenient way to pass information to Arafat.

While based in Tunis, Arafat also spent time in Iraq. He found an ally in Iraqi president Saddam Hussein, who made facilities available to the PLO. For a while, Arafat lived in Baghdad, Iraq. As he told guests who expressed surprise at the simplicity of his surroundings, "I can't live in a comfortable house while I have this job to do for my people."

DECLARATION OF A STATE

In November 1988, the Palestine National Council declared a Palestinian state in Israeli territory that had been occupied by Palestinians before the war of 1967. The PNC also stated that they would accept a two-state solution such as the one proposed in UN Resolution 242.

The declaration had little practical impact. However, by accepting the idea of partition into two states, the statement paved the way for Arafat's second appearance at the United Nations. But this time, the U.S. government refused to grant Arafat a visa to allow him into the country. In response, the United Nations took the unusual step of inviting Arafat to address the General Assembly in Geneva, Switzerland. At huge expense, all the delegates traveled to Geneva from New York—just so that Arafat could be allowed the formal platform to address the United Nations.

The speech, which took place on December 13, 1988, provided Arafat with another opportunity to explain why the Palestinian people felt they had the right to claim a state on land occupied by Israel. One of the themes in his speech was his vision of a Palestine where Jews and Muslims lived side by side. He claimed that Judaism was part of Palestinian heritage and tradition. He expanded on this idea in an interview that same year, saying "We [Jews and Palestinian Muslims] were living together once. The Jews participated in our civilization, in our life, and they were a part of us and we were a part of them as a nation. Throughout our history there are famous Jews of Arab stock."

In that same interview, he pointed the finger of blame for the ongoing conflict squarely at the United States. "If the [U.S.] administration . . . deals with the rights of five million Palestinians we will be on the right road for peace," Arafat said.

But U.S. leaders made it clear that they would only deal with the PLO if it publicly renounced violence, without qualification or reservation. Arafat did not make such a commitment during his UN speech. Only during a press conference that followed did he finally utter the words that the U.S. government wanted to hear. Clearly uncomfortable to be put on the spot, he said in English—though never in Arabic—"I repeat for the record that we totally and absolutely renounce terrorism." While some observers found this announcement promising, most doubted that Arafat would keep his promises.

In April 1989, the PNC elected Arafat as president of Palestine, despite the fact that Palestine was still a state without territory. In May Arafat made an official visit to Paris. He enlisted Suha Tawil to help with the arrangements. Suha was someone who could stand up to Yasser Arafat. While others became frightened when he got angry, she was never cowed into submission. She didn't like it when he lost his temper, and she found a way to make sure that he kept control of it. As she told it, "When I was his assistant I used to give Arafat only the very important papers. Sometimes the news in them was not good. On these occasions, I would stand in front of him with the papers in my hand and I would say, 'Abu Amar [Arafat's code name], I am not going to give you these papers unless you promise me that you will not shout and scream when you read them.'"

A Secret Marriage

The relationship between Arafat and Suha eventually developed beyond work. Suha said, "It was not love at first sight, but there was a chemistry. I felt there was something in Abu Amar's eyes for me." During one of Suha's many visits to Tunis, Yasser Arafat proposed to her. However, he imposed one condition: no one other than close family and friends must know that they were married. Arafat was then sixty and Suha twenty-six years old. They were married on July 17, 1990, in the front room of Arafat's house in Tunis.

Arafat is likely to have kept his marriage a secret because he was uncomfortable with the idea of being married. He had always said that he was "married to

Yasser Arafat and his wife, Suha

the cause" and had no time for a real marriage. He also may have thought that the announcement of their marriage would be a distraction during the intifada, when many Palestinians were grieving for loved ones who had been killed.

In addition, Arafat had never seemed to be much of a family man. He portrayed the image of a loner, a highly independent person who was happy living by himself. At the same time, he professed to love being around children. Every Ramadan (a holy month in the Islamic calendar), he visited children in orphanages to share meals with them and to give them presents.

Suha remained down-to-earth about their lives and marriage. She told one of Arafat's biographers, Alan Hart, "Abu Amar is the symbol of the regeneration of Palestinian nationalism. His wife is not the symbol. I am married to the symbol, but I don't treat him as the symbol. My relationship is with the man, the person, the human being, and this perhaps is why he thought we would make a good couple." Suha was obliged to make many sacrifices. Her new husband was accustomed to working very long days. He only slept for a couple of two-hour stretches in the early morning and late afternoon. He never ate at restaurants, partly because it would have been too dangerous but mostly because he was not interested in doing so. He was never happier than when he was working: writing letters, sending and receiving faxes, making numerous telephone calls, meeting a regular stream of visitors, and frequently traveling abroad for face-to-face meetings with world leaders.

ISOLATION AND BAD CHOICES

In August 1990, Iraq invaded its tiny neighbor Kuwait. Arafat was faced with a dilemma. Did he condemn this aggressive invasion, as almost every Arab state had done, or did he support it? Usually, when faced with such difficult decisions, Arafat did not reveal his thinking one way or the other. But in this instance, he openly chose to support Iraqi president Saddam Hussein, who had always been a loyal supporter of the PLO. Arafat also attempted to mediate between Iraq and Kuwait, but without success.

Meanwhile, a U.S.-led coalition including Arab nations in the region assembled to expel Iraq from Kuwait. This conflict became known as the Gulf War. Arafat declared that the Palestinians would fight alongside their Iraqi brothers. After Iraq lost the Gulf War, Arafat, like Saddam Hussein, was labeled by many nations as a dangerous aggressor. Almost overnight, funding for the PLO from Arab countries dried up. Arafat was shunned and isolated.

A U.S. marine stands guard over an Iraqi soldier taken prisoner during the Gulf War. Arafat's support for Saddam Hussein in this conflict led to a loss of support for the PLO on the world stage.

In 1991 U.S. president George H. W. Bush arranged a new set of negotiations to initiate an Arab-Israeli peace process. The Arab states had made it clear that, in exchange for supporting the United States in the Gulf War, they expected progress on the resolution of the Palestinian issue. The parties involved in the October 1991 negotiations, which were held in Madrid, Spain, were Israel, Syria, Lebanon, and a joint Palestinian-Jordanian delegation. Although the meetings made limited progress, plans were made for future talks.

But during a new round of talks in 1992, Palestinian negotiators nearly found themselves without a leader. Arafat, whose life had been filled with near escapes, suddenly had his closest brush with death yet. In April 1992, the light plane in which he was a passenger ran out of fuel in the middle of a sandstorm and made a crash landing in the Libyan desert. For many hours, no

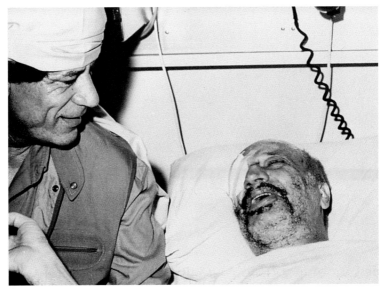

Libyan leader Muammar Qaddafi, left, visits Arafat, right, in a hospital in Amman, Jordan, following a plane crash on April 29, 1992.

one knew where the plane was or whether Arafat was dead or alive. In desperation, one of Arafat's assistants appealed to former U.S. president Jimmy Carter for help. Recognizing that Arafat's presence could be critical to the success of the peace negotiations, the U.S. government gave the order for American satellites to track down the missing plane. Arafat was found and rushed to a hospital in Amman, Jordan, with a blood clot on the brain. The plane's pilot and two others were killed in the crash, but Arafat survived. His luck had saved him again.

Arafat, right, shakes the hand of Israeli prime minister Yitzhak Rabin, left, after signing the Oslo Accords on September 13, 1993. U.S. president Bill Clinton, center, looks on.

Chapter **SEVEN**

ONE STEP FORWARD, TWO STEPS BACK

WHILE THE MADRID NEGOTIATIONS OF 1991 HAD appeared to lead nowhere, another avenue soon opened. The initiative for a new series of negotiations came from Norway, a country in northern Europe that was neutral in the dispute. Norway has a tradition of peacemaking and encouraging international cooperation. More importantly, the talks were kept completely secret. The organizers of the negotiations hoped that being out of the glare of worldwide publicity might offer the negotiating parties a better chance for coming to a compromise. The discussions, which were held in Oslo, Norway, and attended by representatives of Israel and the PLO, became known as the Oslo Channel.

An Agreement, At Last

An agreement between Israel and the PLO was finally reached in Oslo, something that had not been achieved since the founding of Israel. Israel agreed to recognize the PLO, remove troops from the Gaza Strip and Jericho (a town in the West Bank), and give the Palestinians limited self-rule in the city of Jericho and other parts of the West Bank. A handover of control would take place over a period of five years. In return, the Palestinians agreed to recognize the state of Israel, to cease making claims to Israeli territory, and to stop Palestinian violence completely.

But in the Palestinians' eyes, some important issues were still left unresolved. First and foremost, the agreement, known as the Oslo Accords, did not establish a completely independent Palestinian state. The Palestinian side expected this issue to be the subject of future negotiations. Secondly, no agreement on the size of the territory to be handed over to the Palestinians had been reached. Other key matters that were not addressed were the return of Palestinians living in refugee camps, the future of Jewish settlements, and the future of the city of Jerusalem, which both Israel and Palestine regarded as an integral part of their states.

Nevertheless, many observers hoped that peace was on the way at last. On September 9, Arafat sent a letter to Rabin stating that the PLO recognized Israel and renounced violence. Rabin also sent a letter to Arafat, recognizing the PLO.

The final signing of the Oslo Accords took place at the White House in Washington, D.C., on September 13, 1993, with U.S. president Bill Clinton acting as the mediator. With the world's media in attendance, Arafat thrust out his hand toward Rabin. Rabin—who, in the past, had refused to shake Arafat's hand—paused for a moment. Then he stretched out his own hand. It was one of history's most famous handshakes.

With the ceremony over, not everyone within the Palestinian leadership approved of the agreement. Many people felt that Arafat had made too many concessions to the Israelis without securing absolute guarantees on two important issues: the recognition of a Palestinian state and the end of Jewish settlements. Arafat replied to his critics that the Palestinians had to seize the opportunity of compromise. "At certain historical moments, it is the duty and the responsibility of leaders to lead. In critical moments the decision must be taken. When the decisions have been taken it is up to the collective leadership to wait and judge the leader on the basis of his results." He was criticized by, among others, Mahmoud Darwish, a member of the executive committee of the PLO. Darwish resigned after the Oslo Accords, saying that Arafat was embarking on an ill-advised adventure. Arafat replied, "All my life has been a historical adventure."

Arafat had many reasons for signing the accords. The intifada had led to much death and misery. Thousands of Palestinians had been killed, wounded, detained, or arrested. Many Israelis had also been injured and killed. Secondly, the PLO was so short of money that it may have had no choice but to make a deal with Israel. After the Gulf War, the flow of funds to the PLO had almost dried up. Many observers thought that the PLO was actually bankrupt. A third reason may have been that Arafat, who liked to be in control, was in a very weak position and in danger of losing his status as a leader. He may have hoped that a dramatic gesture might restore his authority. Signing an agreement with Israel provided just that. One political commentator described the situation in these terms: "Oslo was a lifebelt for Arafat. Without it, he would have drowned."

The agreement angered many in Israel, too. On February 25, 1994, a lone Israeli gunman entered a mosque in the town of Hebron. He killed twenty-nine worshippers and wounded many others, before he himself was killed by Muslim witnesses.

Despite the protests and the new turmoil, Israel and the PLO initially kept the promises of the Oslo Accords. On May 4, 1994, an additional agreement was signed in Cairo. In this document, Israel agreed to withdraw from parts of the Gaza Strip, including the city of Jericho.

RETURNING HOME

Two months later, Arafat entered Gaza in triumph, to the wild acclaim of hundreds of thousands of residents. He kissed the ground on arrival and set up PLO

Crowds celebrate Arafat's return to Gaza in July 1994.

headquarters in the former British governor's house. It was the first time he had been on official Palestinian soil in more than twenty years. Arafat also established a new body within the Palestinian government, called the Palestinian National Authority (PNA). The PNA was responsible for governing Palestinian areas that had been granted self-rule.

In October 1994, Arafat, Rabin, and the Israeli foreign minister Shimon Peres were jointly awarded the Nobel Peace Prize for their efforts to bring peace to the Middle East. In the speech that Arafat made when accepting the award, he said, "As war is an adventure, peace is also a challenge and a gamble."

Yasser Arafat, right, receives the 1994 Nobel Peace Prize from Francis Sejersted, left, chairman of the Nobel Committee. The ceremony took place in Oslo, Norway, in October 1994.

Adding to Arafat's joy was the birth of his daughter in the summer of 1995. He and Suha named the baby Zahwa, after Arafat's mother.

Peace negotiations continued into 1995, with further agreements by Israel to withdraw from occupied territory and to allow Palestinian elections. On September 24, 1995, Arafat and Shimon Peres signed an agreement referred to as Oslo II. Oslo II divided the West Bank into three zones. The PNA would be given control over civil affairs in Zone A. Zone B was placed under joint Israeli-Palestinian control, and Zone C remained under Israeli control.

But peace was still very fragile. Some Palestinians were determined to continue the fight and to carry out extreme measures in pursuit of their aims. On October 19, a Palestinian suicide bomber belonging to the Hamas group blew himself up in a bus in Tel Aviv, Israel. The attack killed more than twenty Israelis and injured dozens of others. On November 4, an Israeli extremist who was opposed to any agreement with the

Palestinians assassinated Rabin, sending shock waves through the region.

In Israel, it was not only extremists who opposed the agreement with Arafat. In May 1996, the Israeli Labor Party lost the general election to the more conservative Likud Party, which had traditionally taken a stance more hostile to the PLO. The leader of the Likud Party, and the new prime minister, was Benjamin Netanyahu. He accused Arafat of failing to implement the Oslo agreements by not combating terrorism.

Despite Netanyahu's objections, progress in the negotiations continued. The two men signed an important agreement in early 1997, under which Israel agreed to remove its troops from most of Hebron, the last occupied city in the West Bank. In October 1998, the Wye River Memorandum scheduled further Israeli withdrawals from the rest of the West Bank and from Gaza.

May 1999 had been set as the deadline for implementing all the points agreed upon in Oslo in 1993. But the deadline came and went, and both sides

Suha Arafat, Yasser's wife, holds their baby daughter, Zahwa.

seemed unable to bring matters to a conclusion. Meanwhile, another change of prime minister in Israel took place in the summer of 1999. The Labor Party leader Ehud Barak defeated Netanyahu in elections to become prime minister. Barak agreed with Arafat to set a date of September 13, 2000, for a final peace settlement based on the Oslo Accords. This deadline, too, passed without action. Barak offered almost all of the territory of the West Bank in "full and final settlement," but Arafat refused the proposal, insisting that the Palestinian side had already conceded more than enough and would accept nothing less than all of the West Bank.

If Arafat had found it difficult to negotiate with Barak, the election of Ariel Sharon as his successor as prime minister in February 2001 made compromise even less likely. Many Israelis saw Arafat's rejection of Barak's proposal as a clear indication that Arafat was not as interested in peace as he claimed. These Israeli citizens supported Sharon, a hard-line former general, in the next elections. Sharon had a history of leading military campaigns against the Palestinians, including the Israeli invasion of southern Lebanon in 1982. In September 2000, he had inflamed an already tense situation by staging a very public visit to the Temple Mount (called al-Haram al-Sharif in Arabic). The site is regarded as sacred to both Muslims and Jews. The Palestinians saw this act as provocative, and shortly afterward a second intifada began in the West Bank and Gaza. Some people believe that the second intifada had been planned before Sharon's visit, while others think that Sharon's visit to the Temple Mount was the spark. In any case, renewed violence erupted and showed no signs of slowing.

After Sharon's election, he stated that he would only agree to a Palestinian territory—with no mention at all of self-rule—comprising about 50 percent of the West Bank and 60 percent of the Gaza Strip. This proposal was utterly unacceptable to the Palestinian leadership.

CAUGHT IN THE MIDDLE

During this period, Arafat's authority was increasingly challenged and weakened. He found himself caught between two forces. The Israeli government regarded him as a terrorist incapable of stemming the latest spate of devastating suicide bombings, which were carried out both by members of PLO factions and by Palestinians acting alone. On the other side, militant Palestinians felt no nearer to achieving a settled homeland. Violence escalated. In 2002 the Israeli army trapped Arafat in his headquarters in Ramallah, in a siege that ended after five weeks. Arafat's leadership was increasingly marginalized. Seeing him as both ineffective and corrupt, many Palestinian groups took matters into their own hands.

In the summer of 2002, U.S. president George W. Bush said that a settlement of the half-century-long dispute between Israel and the Palestinians would only be

Palestinians in Gaza run to escape tear gas during clashes with Israeli troops during the second intifada.

resolved by new Palestinian leadership. In other words, the U.S. government wanted Yasser Arafat removed as head of the PLO. But that raised a big, unresolved question: If not Arafat, who?

ARAFAT, THE ORATOR

When he speaks in English, Yasser Arafat often talks in a halting, stilted manner. But when he speaks in his mother tongue, Arabic, he is a fiery orator, capable of rousing an audience to great excitement.

He is blessed with a superb memory, remembering people, places, and events upon which he draws in his speeches. He can also find colorful words to describe the plight of the Palestinians. Here is a selection of his quotes, translated from Arabic into English.

"Heartbeat by heartbeat, hand by hand, we'll build a new era."

"I am a rebel and freedom is my cause."

"[The causes of the Palestinian conflict] do not stem from any conflict between two religions or two nationalisms. Neither is it a border conflict between neighboring states. It is the cause of a people deprived of its homeland, dispersed and uprooted, and living mostly in exile and in refugee camps."

"As war is an adventure, peace is also a challenge and a gamble."

"The difference between the revolutionary and the terrorist lies in the reason for which each fights. For whoever stands by a just cause and fights for the freedom and liberation of his land from the invaders cannot be called terrorist."

Arafat talks to reporters in Gaza.

EPILOGUE

Time is catching up with Yasser Arafat. In his seventies, he suffers from Parkinson's disease, a degenerative disease of the nervous system. Years of hard work and struggle have taken their toll. He has to take many different medications, which he carries with him in a sandwich box. His wife and daughter spend most of their time far away, for safety reasons. The sparkle in his eyes has dimmed. When he appears on television, he often seems weary and low in spirits.

Yet Arafat remains a fighter. For more than thirty years, he has led his movement with undeniable forcefulness. He gets along with most people whom he meets, has personal charisma, and is a masterful public speaker. He knows how to win—and buy—loyalty. And he believes that he knows what the Palestinian people want and need. Many people believe that, so long as there is breath in his body, he will battle on for his vision of the Palestinian cause. And Arafat has nearly paid for his commitment with his life on many occasions. He wears body protection and a bulletproof vest every time he goes out. Both of his closest partners in the Palestinian cause, Khalil Wazir and Salah Khalaf, have been assassinated.

Arafat also fears failure. He longs to be the man who brings the dream of a Palestinian homeland to reality. However, even if some kind of peace is reached in the

Palestinian-Israeli conflict, it is becoming less and less likely that Arafat himself will achieve it. By 2003, with the terrorism and bloodshed continuing day after day, both the Israeli and the U.S. governments had strengthened their calls for his removal, refusing to continue dealing with him politically or diplomatically. In March 2003, Mahmoud Abbas (also known as Abu Mazen)—a founding member of Fatah and a prominent Palestinian figure—was chosen as Palestinian prime

Arafat and new Palestinian prime minister Mahmoud Abbas

minister. This change in leadership is designed to reduce Arafat's influence and, hopefully, to insure the success of a peace deal. In the spring and summer of 2003, peace talks took place among Abbas, Ariel Sharon, and international leaders including U.S. and Egyptian officials. Palestinian terrorist groups agreed to a cease-fire in July, and Israel likewise agreed to take steps toward a Palestinian state. However, peace is still fragile. In addition, many observers believe that Arafat will never loosen his grip on power and that he will continue to pull strings from behind the scenes no matter what happens.

And, no matter what happens, Arafat will be a tough act to follow. He remains a highly popular leader with many Palestinians. He dispenses funds and grants favors so skillfully that many people are deeply indebted to him. He is widely admired for his unstinting efforts in the Palestinian cause. So far as is known, he is untainted by political corruption or scandal. Although some reports indicate that he has millions of dollars in a secret bank account, Arafat carefully portrays himself as a man who genuinely puts his life's work ahead of personal gain. His has been a remarkable life by any measure. If and when the state of Palestine is created, it will owe much to Yasser Arafat.

SOURCES

11 Alan Hart, *Arafat* (London: Sidgwick & Jackson, 1994),
14.

17 David Hirst, *The Gun and the Olive Branch: The Roots of
Violence in the Middle East* (London: Faber & Faber,
1984), 38.

33–34 Ibid., 270.

34 Andrew Gowers and Tony Walker, *Behind the Myth:
Yasser Arafat and the Palestinian Revolution* (New York:
Olive Branch Press, 1992), 62.

41 Hart, *Arafat*, 205.

44–45 Ibid., 217.

61 Hirst, *The Gun and the Olive Branch*, 333.

62 Ibid., 335.

83 Morgan Strong, "The Playboy Interview: Yasir Arafat,"
Playboy Magazine, September 1988.

84 Ibid.

84 Ibid.

84 Gowers and Walker, *Behind the Myth*, 299.

85 Hart, *Arafat*, 529.

85 Ibid., 516.

86 Ibid., 519.

93 Ibid., xxvii-xxviii.

93 Said K. Aburish, *Arafat: From Defender to Dictator*
(London: Bloomsbury, 1998), 256.

94 Confidential source, conversation with author, London
(July 4, 2002).

95 "PLO Chairman Arafat—Nobel Prize for Peace," *Israeli
Ministry of Foreign Affairs*, n.d,
<http://www.mfa.gov.il/mfa/go.asp?MFAH00th0>
(December 4, 2002).

101 Confidential source, conversation with author, London
(July 4, 2002).

101 "Statement by H. E. Mr. Yasser Arafat Chairman of the
     Palestine Liberation Organization before the 29th
     Session of the United Nations General Assembly 13
     November 1974," *Palestine-UN.org*, n.d.,
     <http://www.palestine-un.org/mission/3a_29.html>
     (December 4, 2002).
101 Ibid.
101 "PLO Chairman Arafat," *Israeli Ministry of Foreign
     Affairs*.
101 "Statement by H. E. Mr. Yasser Arafat," *Palestine-UN.org*.

SELECTED BIBLIOGRAPHY

Aburish, Said K. *Arafat: From Defender to Dictator.* London: Bloomsbury, 1998.

Downing, David. *Yasser Arafat.* Oxford: Heinemann Library, 2002.

Gowers, Andrew, and Tony Walker. *Behind the Myth: Yasser Arafat and the Palestinian Revolution.* New York: Olive Branch Press, 1992.

Hart, Alan. *Arafat.* London: Sidgwick & Jackson, 1994.

Hirst, David. *The Gun and the Olive Branch: The Roots of Violence in the Middle East.* London: Faber and Faber, 1984.

Wallach, Janet, and John Wallach. *Arafat in the Eyes of the Beholder.* Secaucus, NJ: Birch Lane Press, 1997.

FOR FURTHER READING

Corzine, Phyllis. *The Palestinian-Israeli Accord.* San Diego: Lucent Books, 1997.

Ferber, Elizabeth. *Yasir Arafat: A Life of War and Peace.* Brookfield, CT: Millbrook Press, 1995.

Goldstein, Margaret J. *Israel in Pictures.* Minneapolis, MN: Lerner Publications Company, 2004.

Katz, Samuel M. *Jerusalem or Death: Palestinian Terrorism.* Minneapolis, MN: Lerner Publications Company, 2004.

Sha'ban, Mervet Akram, and Galit Fink. *If You Could Be My Friend: Letters of Mervet Akram Sha'ban and Galit Fink.* New York: Orchard Books, 1998.

Slavik, Diane. *Daily Life in Ancient and Modern Jerusalem.* Minneapolis, MN: Runestone Press, 2001.

Wagner, Heather Lehr. *Israel and the Arab World.* Philadelphia: Chelsea House, 2002.

INDEX

OTHER TITLES FROM LERNER AND A&E®:

Arthur Ashe

The Beatles

Benjamin Franklin

Bill Gates

Bruce Lee

Carl Sagan

Chief Crazy Horse

Christopher Reeve

Colin Powell

Daring Pirate Women

Edgar Allan Poe

Eleanor Roosevelt

George W. Bush

George Lucas

Gloria Estefan

Jack London

Jacques Cousteau

Jane Austen

Jesse Owens

Jesse Ventura

Jimi Hendrix

John Glenn

Latin Sensations

Legends of Dracula

Legends of Santa Claus

Louisa May Alcott

Madeleine Albright

Malcolm X

Mark Twain

Maya Angelou

Mohandas Gandhi

Mother Teresa

Nelson Mandela

Oprah Winfrey

Osama bin Laden

Princess Diana

Queen Cleopatra

Queen Elizabeth I

Queen Latifah

Rosie O'Donnell

Saddam Hussein

Saint Joan of Arc

Thurgood Marshall

Tiger Woods

William Shakespeare

Wilma Rudolph

Women in Space

Women of the Wild West

ABOUT THE AUTHOR

George Headlam has written extensively about developing world issues and traveled in that capacity to countries in the Middle East and Asia. He currently works as a professional writer, living with his wife and two children in London.

PHOTO ACKNOWLEDGMENTS

Photographs used with permission of: Popperfoto, pp. 2 (Sven Nackstrand), 12, 22, 25, 29, 36, 39, 41, 42, 48, 53, 54, 56 (UPI), 58, 63, 67, 72, 86 (Fayez Nureldin), 90, 95, 96 (Menahem Kahana), 97; Popperfoto/Reuters, pp. 6 (Hussein Hussein), 9 (Laszlo Balogh), 10 (Hussein Hussein), 15 (Mahfouz Abu Turk), 100 (Reinhard Krause), 102 (Suhaib Salem), 104 (© Reuters NewMedia Inc./CORBIS); Camera Press, pp. 30 (Terence Spencer), 69 (Rachad El Koussy); Topham Picturepoint, pp. 34, 37, 50, 74, 75 (AP), 80 (AP), 88 (ImageWorks); Rex/TimePix, pp. 49, 64 (Michael Evans), 71 (Dirck Halstead); Rex/Sipa Press, p. 89.

Cover photos for hard cover and soft cover: front, © Georges Merillon/ GAMMA/ZUMA Press; back, Munib al-Masri.

WEBSITES

The website addresses (URLs) included in this book were valid at the time of printing. However, because of the nature of the Internet, it is possible that some addresses may have changed, or sites may have changed or closed down since publication. While the author, packager and Publisher regret any inconvenience this may cause readers, no responsibility for any such changes can be accepted by the author, packager, or Publisher.